12/15

DIEGO RIVERA

*Famous Mexican
Painter*

Mateo Alvarez

 Enslow Publishing
101 W. 23rd Street
Suite 240
New York, NY 10011
USA

enslow.com

Words to Know

academy—A school that teaches special subjects, such as art, music, or dance.

landscape—A picture of countryside or a scene in nature.

mural—A large work of art on a wall or ceiling.

plaster—A paste that hardens and is used to coat walls.

portrait—A picture of a person.

revolution—Overthrowing the government to put new leaders in place.

scholarship—Money given by a school to help pay for education.

still life—A picture of objects, such as fruit or plants.

tall tales—Stories that are not true.

Contents

Words to Know 2

CHAPTER 1 Early Days 5

CHAPTER 2 A Time of Change 9

CHAPTER 3 Bringing Murals to America 14

CHAPTER 4 The Pride of Mexico.............18

Timeline............................22

Learn More 23

Index 24

Diego Rivera

Early Days

Diego Rivera was born on December 8, 1886, in the Mexican town of Guanajuato. His parents, María and Diego de Rivera, were schoolteachers. He had a twin brother named Carlos. When Diego was only a year and a half old, his brother died. Carlos had always been a sick child. It was a very sad time for the family.

For the next two years, Diego often stayed with his babysitter, Antonia, in her village in the mountains.

At home, he lived with his mother, father, and two aunts. In 1891, his baby sister, María, was born.

Art Student

As a little boy, Diego loved to draw. He often drew all over the walls and furniture in his home. Finally, his father gave him a special room covered with paper. Diego was allowed to draw on anything in that room.

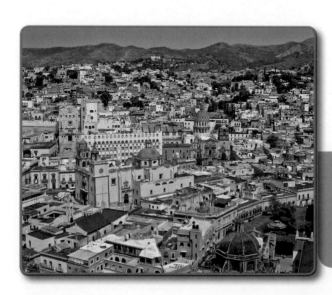

Diego lived in the city of Guanajuato when he was a young boy.

Guanajuato is 176 miles (284 kilometers) from Mexico City.

When Diego was almost seven, his family moved to Mexico City. At age ten, he started taking evening classes at Mexico's national school of art, the San Carlos **Academy**. After a year, he stopped going to regular school. Instead he went to the San Carlos Academy every day.

Everyone saw that Diego had a lot of talent. He was one of the best students in the school and graduated with high honors. He was given a **scholarship** to study art in Europe. In 1907, Diego left Mexico to learn more about painting. He was twenty years old.

Diego Says:

"Great art is like a tree, which grows in a particular place and has a trunk, leaves . . . and roots of its own."

CHAPTER 2

A Time of Change

In Europe, Diego learned about all different kinds of art. He traveled to Spain, France, and other countries, meeting artists and painting pictures. He tried different styles of painting. He painted **landscapes**, **portraits**, and **still lifes**.

While Diego was in Europe, the Mexican **Revolution** began back home. The war started because the poor people of Mexico wanted better lives. It lasted for ten years. By the time Diego returned home in 1921, his country had changed.

Diego the Storyteller

The new leaders of Mexico believed that art was for all its people—rich and poor. So they asked artists to paint **murals** on the walls of buildings. Diego liked this idea because the pictures in a mural can tell a story. Many Mexicans could not read. Diego's murals were a way to teach them about Mexico's history and heroes.

In 1922, Diego started his first mural. Painting a mural was hard work. Sometimes Diego worked

Emiliano Zapata was a leader in the Mexican Revolution. Diego painted many pictures about the war.

for more than twelve hours straight. When he painted a mural, the **plaster** on the wall had to be wet. He had to finish painting before it dried.

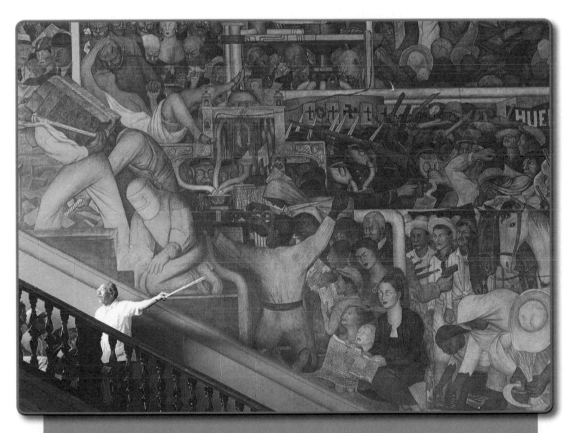

Diego's mural, *The History of Mexico*, can be seen at the National Palace in Mexico City.

People liked to watch Diego work, and he liked to tell them stories about his life. Some of the stories were true. Some were **tall tales**. Diego was famous for his stories and his wild imagination.

The government asked Diego to paint murals in the National Palace. On the staircase, Diego painted the history of Mexico. Other walls showed the temples, palaces, and Indian gods from long ago. Diego wanted the Mexican people to be proud of their history.

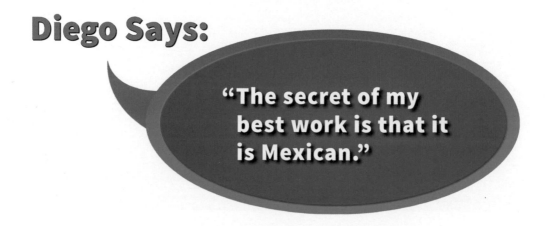

Diego Says:

"The secret of my best work is that it is Mexican."

Diego's murals were very large and sometimes took years to complete.

CHAPTER 3

Bringing Murals to America

After he returned to Mexico, Diego met an art student named Frida Kahlo. Several years later, they met again, and soon they fell in love. They married on August 21, 1929.

Diego was becoming famous. People in the United States asked him to visit and paint murals there. In 1930, Diego and Frida traveled to California and then to New York City. There, the Museum of Modern Art put on a big show of more than a hundred of his paintings. It was a success.

Diego loved the machines and factories that he saw in Detroit. This mural is called *Detroit Industry*.

Diego and Frida also went to Detroit, Michigan, a busy city with big factories making cars. Machines had always fascinated Diego. He loved to watch them move and make noise. For his murals in Detroit, he painted people working in the factories with big machines, pipes, and motors.

Frida Kahlo was an artist who was known for her self-portraits.

Diego Says:

"**Frida had already become the most important fact in my life.**"

A Marriage in Trouble

Diego's wife, Frida, was also a well-known painter, but their work was very different. While he filled huge walls with his art, she painted small portraits of herself. Diego's murals tell stories about Mexico. Most of Frida's paintings are about things that happened in her own life.

Diego loved his wife very much, but he was not always a good husband. Frida and Diego's marriage had many problems. After ten years, they got a divorce.

CHAPTER 4

The Pride of Mexico

In 1940 the city of San Francisco asked Diego to paint a mural about Mexicans and Americans working together. He painted scenes from the past and the present. He included portraits of Mexicans and Americans who worked for freedom.

Diego was unhappy without Frida. She missed him too. On his birthday, December 8, 1940, Diego and Frida married for the second time. He was fifty-four years old.

Diego liked to tell stories with his paintings.

A Lifetime of Art

In 1949 the National Institute of Fine Arts put together a special show of Diego's work. He had been painting for more than fifty years. Diego also collected art made by Indians who lived in Mexico long, long ago. He built his own museum,

Diego's studio was filled with many different kinds of artwork.

called Anahuacalli (ah-nah-wah-CAH-yee), just for this artwork.

Frida died in 1954. Three years later, on November 24, 1957, Diego died of heart failure. He was seventy-one years old. He gave his museum to the Mexican people.

Diego Says:

"The most joyous moments of my life were those I had spent in painting."

Diego Rivera spent most of his life telling stories with his murals. He showed his pride in his country by painting the history and people of Mexico. Today, his stories live on in the artwork that covers the walls of buildings in both America and Mexico.

Timeline

1886—Diego Rivera is born in Guanajuato, Mexico, on December 8.

1893—Diego's family moves to Mexico City.

1907—Diego travels to Europe to study art.

1922—Diego starts painting his first mural.

1929—Diego marries Frida Kahlo, who is also an artist.

1930—Diego paints murals in San Francisco.

1931—Museum of Modern Art in New York City has a special show of his work.

1932—Diego paints murals in Detroit.

1940—Diego paints ten murals in San Francisco. Remarries Frida Kahlo.

1954—Frida Kahlo dies.

1957—Diego dies on November 24.

2011–2012—Diego's murals return to the Museum of Modern Art for a special exhibition.

Learn More

Books

Bojang, Ali Brownlie. *Mexico*. Chicago: Heinemann, 2013.

Fabiny, Sarah. *Who Was Frida Kahlo?* New York: Grosset & Dunlap, 2013.

National Gallery of Art. *An Eye for Art: Focusing on Great Artists and Their Work.* Chicago: Chicago Review Press, 2013.

Rubin, Susan Goldman. *Diego Rivera: An Artist for the People.* New York: Harry N. Abrams, 2013.

Web Sites

diegorivera.com

Includes a biography, pictures of Diego's artworks, and some short videos.

diegorivera.org

Provides quotes, biography, and images of paintings.

riveramural.com

View one of Diego's most famous works and learn more about the artist and about murals.

Index

A

Anahuacalli, 21

D

Detroit, 15

G

Guanajuato, 5

H

history, of Mexico, 10, 12, 21

K

Kahlo, Frida (wife), 14–15, 17, 18, 21

M

Mexican Revolution, 9
Mexico City, 7–8
Museum of Modern Art, 14

N

National Institute of Fine Arts, 20
National Palace, 12

R

Rivera, Carlos (brother), 5
Rivera, Diego
    awards and honors, 8, 14, 20
    childhood, 5–8
    death, 21
    education, 7–8
    Europe, 8, 9
    marriage, 14, 18
    murals, 10–12, 14–15, 17, 18, 21
    United States, 14–15, 18, 21
Rivera, Diego de (father), 5–6
Rivera, María (mother), 5–6
Rivera, María (sister), 6

S

San Carlos Academy, 7–8

Published in 2016 by Enslow Publishing, LLC.
101 W. 23rd Street, Suite 240, New York, NY 10011

Copyright © 2016 by Enslow Publishing, LLC.

All rights reserved.

No part of this book may be reproduced by any means without the written permission of the publisher.

Cataloging-in-Publication Data

Alvarez, Mateo.
Diego Rivera: famous Mexican painter / by Mateo Alvarez.
p. cm.—(Exceptional Latinos)
Includes bibliographical references and index.
ISBN 978-0-7660-6704-2 (library binding)
ISBN 978-0-7660-6702-8 (pbk.)
ISBN 978-0-7660-6703-5 (6-pack)
1. Rivera, Diego, —1886-1957—Juvenile literature. 2. Painters—Mexico—Biography—Juvenile literature. I. Title.
ND259.R5 A484 2016
759.972—d23

Printed in the United States of America

To Our Readers: We have done our best to make sure all Web site addresses in this book were active and appropriate when we went to press. However, the author and the publisher have no control over and assume no liability for the material available on those Web sites or on any Web sites they may link to. Any comments or suggestions can be sent by e-mail to customerservice@enslow.com.

Photo Credits: Alejandra Matiz/Leo Matiz Foundation Mexico/Getty Images, p. 4; AP/Wide World, pp. 10, 11, 13, 15; Enslow Publishers, Inc., p. 7; Ivan Dmitri/Michael Ochs Archives/Getty Images, p. 1 (Diego Rivera); Miguel Tovar/LatinContent/Getty Images, p. 16; roevin/Moment Select/Getty Images, p. 6; Time & Life Pictures/Getty Images, p. 19, 20; Toria/Shutterstock.com (blue background).

Cover Credits: Ivan Dmitri/Michael Ochs Archives/Getty Images (Diego Rivera); Toria/Shutterstock.com (blue background).